Table of Contents

Foreword An Open Letter To My Fellow Wealth Builders 1
Introduction The Problem With Most Real Estate Investing Opportunities 4
Chapter 1 Understanding NNN Investing 7
    The Mechanics of NNN Leases 9
    Advantages of NNN Leases 9
    Evaluating Potential NNN Investments 10
    Lease Terms and Conditions 10
    Market Dynamics and Cap Rates 11
    Building a Diverse NNN Portfolio 11
    The Future of NNN Investing 11
Chapter 2 Recognizing Lucrative NNN Properties 13
    Tenant Creditworthiness: The Engine of Stability 13
    Key Considerations in Location Analysis 14
    Lease Terms and Escalations: Structuring Profitable Agreements 15
    Property Condition and Maintenance: Maintaining High Performance 15
    Market Cap Rates and Trends: Understanding the Investment Landscape 16
    Building a Diverse NNN Portfolio 17
    The Future of NNN Investing 17
Chapter 3 Financing Strategies for NNN Investments 19
    Leverage and Loan Options: Fueling Your Investment Engine 20
    Understanding Loan Terms and Interest Rates 22
    Maximizing Benefits with 1031 Exchange 26
    Finding the Best Financial Strategy for You 27
Chapter 4 Understanding The Different Types Of NNN Tenants 28
    The Strategic Importance of National Tenants 28
    The Advantages of National, Corporate-Backed Tenants 33

Chapter 5 Embrace Zero Landlord Responsibilities 35

The Core Concept of NNN Leases 35

What Does "Zero Landlord Responsibilities" Really Mean? 36

Practical Scenarios of Zero Responsibilities 37

The Bigger Picture 37

Embracing the Benefits of NNN Investments 38

The Role of Strategic Partnerships 38

Case Studies: Successful NNN Investments 39

Maximizing Returns with NNN Investments 39

Chapter 6 Investment Grade Tenants vs. Non-Investment Grade Tenants 41

The Importance of Tenant Grades 41

Investment Grade Tenants 41

Non-Investment Grade Tenants 43

The Role of a Mentor 44

Real-World Example 44

Chapter 7 Advanced Concepts and Future Steps in NNN Investing 46

Flipping NNN Properties Using Short-Term Leases 46

The Power of Tenant Relationships 47

Dark Sites Investment Strategy 47

Building Relationships and Strategic Partnerships 47

The Role of Mentorship in Advanced NNN Strategies 47

Example Scenarios of Advanced Strategies 48

Future Steps in NNN Investing 48

Conclusion: Transforming Your Portfolio 49

Conclusion Seizing Control in the World of NNN Investing 50

Foreword

An Open Letter To My Fellow Wealth Builders

If you're seeking a way to generate truly passive income, you've picked the right book. But before we dive into the specifics, let me share a tale about my mentor and how I stumbled upon the powerful world of Triple Net (NNN) properties.

Picture this: a few years ago, I found myself in a riveting conversation with a wealthy investor who had a keen interest in NNN properties. It was one of those lightbulb moments that made me realize just how far I'd come and how much further I could go.

My journey didn't commence in the realm of real estate—it kicked off on the football field as a professional quarterback. The transition from sports to real estate wasn't exactly seamless, but it was serendipitous. A friend, recognizing my potential, generously funded my pursuit of a real estate license. This leap of faith was the catalyst for a dramatic career transformation.

Enter Dan Lem, my mentor, and the Gandalf to my Frodo. Dan's wisdom and guidance illuminated the quickest path to acquiring my first NNN property. This wasn't just a minor pivot; it was a revelation. I discovered that true freedom in real estate lies in offloading the burdens that typically weigh investors down. NNN investments promised fewer headaches and more predictable returns—an "Aha!" moment that changed my trajectory entirely.

Unlike your typical broker, I am both a NNN property owner and a mentor. I'm here to guide you toward the financial liberation I discovered. Most real estate ventures are unpredictable—taxes, maintenance, unruly tenants. But NNN properties? They're a breath of fresh air. Imagine owning a property where established businesses like CVS or AutoZone handle taxes, insurance, and maintenance. That's the beauty of NNN investments.

As we navigate through the upcoming chapters, I'll share the secrets to maneuvering the NNN landscape, selecting the right properties, and negotiating terms that secure your future. We'll delve into strategies that transformed my life and can potentially revolutionize yours.

Let's embark on this journey together, a journey that promises enlightenment, stability, and a profitable future.

Now, you might wonder why I'm so enthusiastic about NNN properties. The answer is simple: they are a game-changer. Think of them as the Swiss Army knife of real estate investments—versatile, reliable, and efficient. They strip away the traditional landlord woes and replace them with a steady stream of passive income.

Consider this: in a typical real estate investment, you're constantly juggling taxes, maintenance, and tenant issues. It's a bit like herding cats. But with NNN properties, you hand over those responsibilities to the tenant. They handle the taxes, insurance, and maintenance, leaving you with peace of mind and a reliable income. It's akin to finding a magical goose that lays golden eggs without the usual farmyard mess.

My mentor, Dan Lem, was instrumental in opening my eyes to this world. He wasn't just a mentor; he was a beacon of wisdom in the often murky waters of real estate. Dan taught me that the key to success in NNN properties is not just in acquiring them but in understanding the nuances that make them profitable. From negotiating favorable lease terms to selecting tenants who will uphold their end of the bargain, every detail matters.

And that's what this book is about. It's not just a guide; it's a roadmap to financial freedom. I'll share the insights and strategies that have helped me build a robust portfolio of NNN properties. We'll explore case studies, delve into market analysis, and arm you with the tools you need to make informed decisions.

So, are you ready to transform your financial future? To embrace a real estate strategy that promises less stress and more stability? Then let's get started. Together, we'll navigate the world of NNN properties and uncover the wealth-building opportunities that await.

Get ready for a journey that promises not only financial rewards but also the peace of mind that comes with truly passive income. Welcome to the world of NNN investments—where simplicity meets profitability and where your financial dreams can become a reality.

Introduction
The Problem With Most Real Estate Investing Opportunities

Owning property often means facing challenges that far outweigh the rewards. Every day, the unpredictable elements of property management erode your time and profits, much like termites gnawing at old wood.

This is the stark reality for many real estate investors, who find themselves perpetually grappling with unforeseen expenses, chasing down unreliable tenants, and spending countless hours on emergency repairs. It's a high-maintenance relationship that demands incessant attention and frequently offers minimal returns on that investment of time and effort.

For those who venture into real estate seeking financial freedom and stable passive income, the traditional path can resemble a labyrinth of financial and managerial burdens. From fluctuating rental income and unexpected maintenance costs to the complexities of tenant management, the list of potential headaches is long. The rollercoaster of monthly rent checks and the ever-looming threat of costly vacancies add layers of uncertainty that can deter even the most optimistic investors.

Enter the world of Triple Net Lease (NNN) investments, a strategic pivot in the real estate domain that presents a far more serene landscape. With NNN investments, property owners enjoy the benefits of real estate investment stripped of its most cumbersome aspects. Here, the tenants manage the day-to-day responsibilities that typically fall on the landlord's shoulders—such as property taxes, building insurance, and maintenance.

This shift is not merely about offloading responsibilities; it's a redefinition of the landlord-tenant dynamic. Picture a scenario where your tenant, perhaps a well-known retail chain, handles all the maintenance issues, insurance duties, and property taxes. This is not a typical landlord fantasy. In the NNN investment model, such arrangements are standard, transforming the investment into one with predictable returns, fewer operational headaches, and a significantly more manageable risk profile.

This guide promises more than just an introduction to a different style of investing; it offers a path to reclaiming your time and securing a future where your real estate investments work for you, not the other way around. In the world of NNN investing, you are not merely buying property; you are investing in a streamlined, efficient system that promises to convert your real estate ventures into a portfolio of high-performing assets, minimizing hassle while maximizing financial return. This is real estate investing reimagined—a smarter, more strategic approach that aligns with the goals of modern investors seeking stability and predictability in their real estate endeavors.

Consider this: in traditional real estate investment, you're constantly juggling taxes, maintenance, and tenant issues. It's akin to herding cats. But with NNN properties, those responsibilities shift to the tenant. They handle the taxes, insurance, and maintenance, leaving you with peace of mind and a reliable income. It's like discovering a golden goose that lays eggs without the usual farmyard mess.

My mentor, Dan Lem, was instrumental in opening my eyes to this world. He wasn't just a mentor; he was a beacon of wisdom in the often murky waters of real estate. Dan taught me that the key to success in NNN properties is not just in acquiring them but in understanding the nuances that make them profitable. From negotiating favorable lease terms to selecting tenants who will uphold their end of the bargain, every detail matters.

And that's what this book is about. It's not just a guide; it's a roadmap to financial freedom. I'll share the insights and strategies that have helped me build a robust portfolio of NNN properties. We'll explore case studies, delve into market analysis, and arm you with the tools you need to make informed decisions.

Are you ready to transform your financial future? To embrace a real estate strategy that promises less stress and more stability? Then, let's embark on this journey. Together, we'll navigate the world of NNN properties and uncover the wealth-building opportunities that await.

Chapter 1

Understanding NNN Investing

What if you could take back the helm of your real estate portfolio? No, really, I mean take it back, be in control, and potentially secure a higher return with 99.98% less of the headaches.

As investors and property owners, we often find ourselves overwhelmed with property taxes, landlord responsibilities, property management, unruly tenants, and a slew of other headaches. It's like being constantly bogged down in the daily grind, where your role as an investor becomes more about extinguishing fires than fueling growth.

Enter Triple Net Lease (NNN) investments, a game changer in the world of real estate that offers you a chance to sidestep these disruptions and focus on what really matters: your investment's growth and stability.

NNN investments streamline the landlord experience by shifting the responsibility for property taxes, insurance, and maintenance costs directly to the tenants. Yes, that means you are not responsible for any of those things—it's one hundred percent the tenant's responsibility. There's also a way to ensure that these costs are paid every month for the length of the lease, but I will dive into that a little later.

This isn't just a minor shift in duties—it's a strategic move that changes the entire landscape of property investment. Picture this: owning a commercial property, like a retail building or an office, with tenants such as Hobby Lobby, Starbucks, or even a bank. Imagine having a bank as your tenant with a NNN lease where major operational costs are not your concern. This setup not only frees up your resources but also stabilizes your income, as these costs are no longer variables in your financial planning.

This unique leasing arrangement does more than just offload financial burdens—it infuses your investment strategy with a level of predictability rarely seen in other real estate sectors. With NNN leases, tenants sign long-term agreements, typically ranging from 10 to 25 years. This ensures that you have a steady, uninterrupted cash flow for a substantial period. You're not just investing in real estate; you're investing in a long-term income source with fixed returns, a perfect scenario for those looking to build a robust financial future without daily management hassles.

These properties are not vacant to start with; they already have leases and national tenants. This means the properties cash flow from day one of purchase. The stability of NNN investments is heavily reliant on the caliber of your tenants and the agreement you have with them. A strong tenant—a financially sound and market-tested company—is like a solid foundation for your property investment.

It's crucial to thoroughly vet potential tenants, examining their financial health, market position, and track record. This process ensures that the tenant can meet their lease obligations over the long haul, securing your income stream. Your agreement is only as strong as your tenant; you want a big player, someone whose likelihood of going under is closer to zero than any other number.

Understanding the lease details is another pillar of successful NNN investing. The lease agreement should clearly define all responsibilities and contingencies, covering everything from routine maintenance to major property issues. Knowing exactly what the lease entails helps you anticipate potential challenges and plan accordingly, minimizing surprises that could affect your investment.

Residential prices and returns are often dependent on the economic environment of the market. Prices fluctuate, and rent can fluctuate, but the beauty of NNN leases is their stability over long terms, typically 15 years. Think of NNN as one of the most stable ways of growing your investment. What you see is what you get.

Market dynamics and cap rates also play significant roles in the success of NNN investments. Being aware of the market conditions and economic indicators can help you determine the right time to buy or sell, choose the right properties, and set appropriate lease rates. This kind of market insight allows you to optimize your investment according to current trends and economic cycles, ensuring maximum profitability.

To summarize, NNN investing allows you to step back from day-to-day property management and focus on the broader picture of building wealth through real estate. It's a strategy that reduces operational headaches and provides a predictable, stable income stream, making it an attractive option for investors seeking a more hands-off approach to real estate.

Now, let's dive deeper into the specifics of NNN investing and how it can revolutionize your real estate strategy.

The Mechanics of NNN Leases

At its core, a Triple Net Lease (NNN) is a lease agreement on a property where the tenant agrees to pay all the expenses of the property, including real estate taxes, building insurance, and maintenance. This is in addition to the rent and utilities. The concept is straightforward but profoundly transformative for property owners.

Advantages of NNN Leases

1. **Reduced Landlord Responsibilities**: One of the primary benefits of NNN leases is the significant reduction in the landlord's responsibilities. Traditional leases often require the landlord to handle repairs,

property taxes, and insurance. With NNN leases, these burdens shift to the tenant, allowing you to focus on growing your investment portfolio without being bogged down by day-to-day management tasks.
2. **Predictable Cash Flow**: NNN leases typically come with long-term agreements, ranging from 10 to 25 years. This provides a steady and predictable cash flow, allowing you to plan your financial future with confidence. The stability offered by these long-term leases is invaluable, particularly in uncertain economic times.
3. **Quality Tenants**: NNN properties often attract high-quality tenants, such as national retail chains and established businesses. These tenants are generally more reliable and financially stable, reducing the risk of defaults and vacancies.
4. **Hassle-Free Management**: By transferring the responsibility for property taxes, insurance, and maintenance to the tenant, NNN leases offer a hassle-free management experience. This is particularly beneficial for investors looking to minimize their involvement in the day-to-day operations of their properties.

Evaluating Potential NNN Investments

When considering a NNN investment, it's essential to thoroughly evaluate the potential tenant. This involves examining their financial health, market position, and track record. A financially sound and market-tested tenant is crucial for ensuring the stability and profitability of your investment.

Lease Terms and Conditions

Understanding the lease terms and conditions is vital for successful NNN investing. The lease agreement should clearly define all responsibilities and contingencies, covering everything from routine maintenance to major property issues. This ensures that you are fully aware of what the lease entails and can anticipate potential challenges, minimizing surprises that could affect your investment.

Market Dynamics and Cap Rates

Staying informed about market dynamics and cap rates is crucial for optimizing your NNN investments. Market conditions and economic indicators can help you determine the right time to buy or sell properties, choose the right locations, and set appropriate lease rates. This knowledge allows you to make informed decisions that maximize profitability and ensure the long-term success of your investment portfolio.

Building a Diverse NNN Portfolio

Diversifying your NNN portfolio is another key strategy for mitigating risk and maximizing returns. By investing in a variety of property types and locations, you can spread your risk and ensure a more stable and resilient income stream. This approach allows you to capitalize on different market trends and economic cycles, enhancing the overall performance of your investment portfolio.

The Future of NNN Investing

As the real estate market continues to evolve, NNN investing is likely to become an increasingly attractive option for savvy investors. The combination of reduced management responsibilities, predictable cash flow, and high-quality tenants makes NNN properties a compelling choice for those seeking a more hands-off approach to real estate investing.

NNN investing offers a unique and strategic way to build wealth through real estate. By shifting the burden of property management to the tenant, NNN leases provide a hassle-free and stable income stream, allowing you to focus on the broader picture of growing your investment portfolio. Whether you are a seasoned investor or just starting, NNN investing can help you achieve your financial goals with less stress and more predictability.

Chapter 2
Recognizing Lucrative NNN Properties

Investments can be complicated; often we don't see everything, and it can scare the living bejeebers out of us. The simplicity of NNN investments might put doubts in your mind, so let's dive into the mechanics of how this works to settle any uncertainties.

Here's a crucial note: On any real estate investment, your return is heavily dependent on the person who is paying your rent. The success of NNN investments hinges on several key factors—tenant creditworthiness, strategic location, favorable lease terms, optimal property condition, and an astute awareness of market trends.

Tenant Creditworthiness: The Engine of Stability

Can your tenant pay? This is the most fundamental question for your NNN properties. Engaging tenants with a strong financial foundation and a track record of stability is crucial. These aren't just any tenants; they are often national or multinational companies with proven business models and substantial market presence.

When considering tenants, evaluate them based on several criteria:

- **Credit Rating**: Look for tenants with high credit ratings from reputable agencies such as Moody's, S&P, or Fitch. Ratings in the 'investment grade' spectrum indicate lower risk.
- **Financial Statements**: Analyze balance sheets, income statements, and cash flow statements for profitability, liquidity ratios, and operational efficiency.
- **Market Position and Business Model**: Evaluate the tenant's market share, competitive advantage, and adaptability to market changes.

- **Future Projections**: Consider future earnings projections and industry forecasts. Stable or growing projections indicate a tenant's ability to fulfill long-term lease obligations.

Example: A tenant like CVS Pharmacy, whose corporate-backed lease assures a steady flow of income due to their established business operations and expansive reach.

You might be thinking, "Dennis, this is good and all, but where do I find these tenants?" I'll answer that closer to the end of the book. Before we get there, I want to ensure you have NO doubts that this strategy will work for you. Let's keep going to find out.

Key Considerations in Location Analysis

The location of your NNN property significantly impacts its attractiveness and potential for appreciation. Just as a sports car needs the right balance to maximize performance, your property requires a strategic location to optimize its investment potential.

- **High-Traffic Areas**: Properties located in bustling urban centers or along busy highways naturally attract more business, making them desirable for tenants like fast-food chains or retail stores.
- **Demographics and Trends**: Understanding the local demographics, economic conditions, and competitive landscape is essential. A location thriving with economic activity and a growing population is more likely to sustain a business, thereby securing your rental income.
- **Economic Activity**: Locations with strong economic growth, employment rates, and infrastructure development tend to sustain and attract businesses.
- **Competition**: Assess the competitive landscape. An area with limited direct competition may offer more opportunities for your tenant to thrive.

Lease Terms and Escalations: Structuring Profitable Agreements

Aside from tenant reliability, the lease guarantee behind the lease is equally critical. This is known as a Corporate Guarantee, meaning that even if the tenant fails at that location, they still pay the entire lease agreement. Let's delve into the specifics.

- **Long-Term Leases**: NNN leases typically range from 10 to 25 years, providing a long horizon of stable rental income.
- **Rent Escalations**: To guard against inflation and enhance income growth, rent escalation clauses are essential. These might be fixed annual increases or tied to indexes like the Consumer Price Index (CPI), ensuring that your income keeps pace with economic changes. Sometimes, these increases are done at the 5-year mark, and the structure can vary creatively. The crucial part is ensuring an increase in rent over time.

There are exceptions. Some major retailers might not negotiate. In such cases, revert to the primary rule: Can they pay rent for the next 15 years? If yes, sign the agreement and start collecting your checks. The advantage is that I already have relationships with these companies and understand how they operate. I can hand-deliver these cash-flowing deals if you reach out.

Property Condition and Maintenance: Maintaining High Performance

The upkeep of the property plays a critical role in safeguarding the value of your investment. Like regular maintenance on a sports car, ensuring your property is in top condition is vital for its longevity. Imagine buying a high-end car with a cleaning and maintenance service for its entire lifespan. You never have to clean bird droppings off the window or change the oil or brakes—it's always done for you and in tip-top condition. That's what a NNN lease is to a commercial property owner.

To the point that 50% of my mentees have not even seen their properties, they just get the cash in the bank monthly and know that the agreement is upheld by the corporation.

- **Tenant Responsibilities**: No corporation wants a dirty, filthy place for customers. Statistics show that 87% of people buy from neat and tidy places and spend more in a clean environment. Think about the last time you stepped into a Starbucks—how did that look? In NNN leases, tenants handle major maintenance issues and conduct periodic inspections to ensure compliance and upkeep as per the agreement.
- **Preventive Care**: Routine check-ups prevent major repairs, preserve the property's appeal, and enhance its long-term value, all according to the agreement.

At this point, you might be asking, "What do I do?" The answer is simple: Enjoy your earnings, look for more investments, and leave the rest to the corporate tenant.

Market Cap Rates and Trends: Understanding the Investment Landscape

Let's dive into some terms and concepts that can make or break deals. Understanding capitalization rates (cap rates) and staying attuned to market trends is like having a sophisticated GPS system in your car. These tools guide your investment decisions and strategy.

Cap Rate Insights: A lower cap rate typically indicates a lower-risk investment and can also mean a prime location for real estate. For example, in California, you might own a NNN property with a Starbucks that generates $150,000 in annual rent, resulting in a 4.5% cap rate due to a purchase price of around $3.3 million. In contrast, a similar property in Dallas, Texas, with the same annual rent, would have a 5.5% cap rate and a purchase price of around $2.7 million. California's traffic and location stability justify the higher cost.

By comparing cap rates across different regions and sectors, you can identify properties that offer the best potential returns with acceptable risk levels.

Market Dynamics: Traditional real estate investors need to keep a pulse on economic conditions, real estate cycles, and emerging trends, such as the growth of e-commerce, to adapt their strategies. In NNN, the focus shifts more toward securing corporate guarantees. No need to recognize patterns in commercial real estate to anticipate market shifts—just recognize whether Starbucks or Walmart will be around for the next 15 years.

A primary trend to watch is the state tax system. States like Texas and Florida are income tax-free, which can work in your favor if set up properly. If you'd like more information on this, we have a dedicated team to help our mentees grow and understand these (tax-free) strategies.

Building a Diverse NNN Portfolio

Diversifying your NNN portfolio is crucial for mitigating risk and maximizing returns. By investing in various property types and locations, you can spread risk and ensure a more stable and resilient income stream. This approach allows you to capitalize on different market trends and economic cycles, enhancing the overall performance of your investment portfolio.

The Future of NNN Investing

As the real estate market continues to evolve, NNN investing is likely to become an increasingly attractive option for savvy investors. The combination of reduced management responsibilities, predictable cash flow, and high-quality tenants makes NNN properties a compelling choice for those seeking a more hands-off approach to real estate investing.

In conclusion, NNN investing offers a unique and strategic way to build wealth through real estate. By shifting the burden of property management to the tenant, NNN leases provide a hassle-free and stable income stream, allowing you to focus on the broader picture of growing your investment portfolio. Whether you are a seasoned investor or just starting, NNN investing can help you achieve your financial goals with less stress and more predictability.

Let's embark on this journey together and discover the wealth-building opportunities that NNN investing can offer. Welcome to a smarter, more strategic approach to real estate investing.

Chapter 3
Financing Strategies for NNN Investments

There are a few key lessons I've learned on my journey to building my profile and my clients' portfolios that have been incredibly helpful. In our mentorship program, we do most of this for you since we have it all set up. This opens a loop and ties into our done-for-you offer, ensuring you have a seamless experience.

Knowing your numbers in any investment strategy is crucial. NNN investments are no different; we need to find a way for the strategy to fit into your portfolio and make sure they are backed by reputable financial institutions that verify the numbers make sense.

The goal is to have no debt, except that which is paid by others.

Each financial decision and strategy plays a crucial role in maximizing returns and minimizing the risks associated with taking on debt. In this chapter, we'll delve into the crux of financing options available to you, understand the details of loan terms and interest rates, and explore innovative financing structures like sale-leaseback arrangements and 1031 exchanges.

One fundamental aspect of financing NNN investments is understanding the role of leveraging Other People's Money (OPM). Utilizing borrowed capital to finance a portion of your property's purchase can amplify your potential returns. However, it's essential to navigate this path wisely to maintain a healthy balance between risk and reward. In other words, you want more money coming in than debt going out.

Leverage and Loan Options: Fueling Your Investment Engine

Here are five effective ways to secure financing for your NNN investments:

Traditional Mortgages and Commercial Loans

- **Overview**: Secure a mortgage or commercial loan through banks or financial institutions based on the property's value and your creditworthiness.
- **Benefits**: Access familiar financing structures with potential for favorable terms due to the stability associated with NNN properties.
- **Considerations**: Be diligent in shopping around to secure the best interest rates and terms that align with your investment goals.

SBA Loans

- **Overview**: Utilize Small Business Administration loans to finance commercial properties, benefiting from government-backed assurances.
- **Benefits**: Typically offers lower down payments and more favorable terms compared to conventional bank loans. You can occupy half of the building with your business while an NNN tenant pays for most of the property's expenses.
- **Considerations**: You must own a business to qualify for SBA loans, occupy at least 51% of the property, and meet stringent eligibility criteria.

Example: We worked with a client looking for a building to house a new plastic surgery business. Our team found a beautiful location where Chase Bank was leasing a portion of the building. Chase's rent payments exceeded the new SBA mortgage on the property, giving SBA lenders the confidence they needed to close the deal.

Seller Financing

- **Overview**: Engage in a financing agreement where the property seller extends credit to the buyer with terms between them.
- **Benefits**: Often allows for more flexible terms and can eliminate traditional lending fees. You can get better down payment options and sometimes even better rates.
- **Considerations**: Not all sellers are open or financially able to offer this type of financing, and terms must be carefully negotiated, often incurring higher legal fees.

Our team has already compiled a list of lenders for our mentees to build their NNN portfolios. It typically takes anywhere from 15-35% down for a NNN property, even with seller financing, but we have flexible financiers who we've worked with. These financiers are fantastic to work with, and we have developed ways to cross-collateralize other investments you may have to offset the deposit.

Private Lenders and Hard Money Loans

- **Overview**: Obtain financing from private lenders or through hard money loans, which are typically secured by the property itself.
- **Benefits**: Faster access to capital and less stringent credit requirements.
- **Considerations**: Generally comes with higher interest rates and shorter repayment terms, posing a greater risk.

Each of these options has unique features and potential benefits. Your choice will depend on various factors, including your investment strategy, financial health, and the specific characteristics of the property you intend to acquire.

It's advisable to consult with someone who has experience in NNN investments and the right contacts to ensure everything goes smoothly throughout the purchase process. I've built strategic financial planning steps that I've kept secret for a while, helping many people build a cash-flowing wealth strategy that will last them a lifetime through leveraging the advantages of NNN investments effectively.

Understanding Loan Terms and Interest Rates

The terms of the loan and the nature of the interest rates you commit to can profoundly affect both your immediate cash flow and the long-term profitability of your NNN investment. Knowing these details helps you structure your finances more effectively, especially in other parts of the world:

- **Fixed vs. Variable Interest Rates**: Fixed rates lock you into a consistent rate throughout the loan, shielding you from market fluctuations and making financial forecasting easier. Variable rates might start lower but are subject to change based on economic conditions, potentially increasing your financial burden unexpectedly.
- **Impact on Cash Flow**: Lower interest rates reduce the amount you pay back each month, enhancing your property's cash flow. This is particularly advantageous for NNN properties, where stable, predictable cash flow is a key attraction. Once you have your property, there are many strategies you can use to lower your monthly costs on the mortgage to maximize your monthly income. We help our mentees with multiple strategies to build cash flow as quickly as possible, focusing on long-term planning to maximize the rent schedule.

Example: Let's say that at the 6-year mark, we do a refinancing. This would lower monthly payments and increase the rent, adding a significant return on investment per year due to reduced monthly mortgage payments.

Rent Schedule

Lease Year	Annual	Monthly	Rent PSF	Increase ($/SF)
Year 1 - 5	$135,000	$11,250	$90.24	-
Year 6 - 10	$148,500	$12,375	$99.26	10.0%
Year 11 - 15	$163,350	$13,613	$109.19	10.0%
Year 16 - 20	$179,685	$14,974	$120.11	10.0%
Option 1	$197,654	$16,471	$132.12	10.0%
Option 2	$217,419	$18,118	$145.33	10.0%
Option 3	$239,161	$19,930	$159.87	10.0%

Here is Loan:

Loan Amount	**1,517,750**	Calc
Interest Rate	**6.55**	% per year
Loan Term	**25** Years	Months

Extra Payment Per Month

Reset   Calculate

Monthly Payment: 10,295.43
Total Payment: 3,088,629.00
Total Interest: 1,570,879.00
Annual Payment: 123,545.16
Mortgage Constant: 8.14%

Email   Amortization

Let's say that at the 6-year mark, if we do a refinancing, we would then have a much lower payment and a rent raise, adding close to a $20,000 + return on your investment per year. Due to monthly mortgage payments going from $10,295.43 to $9277.92

Loan Amount	**1,367,750**		Calc
Interest Rate	**6.55**	% per year	
Loan Term	**25** Years		Months
Extra Payment Per Month			

Reset	Calculate

Monthly Payment: 9,277.92
Total Payment: 2,783,376.00
Total Interest: 1,415,626.00
Annual Payment: 111,335.04
Mortgage Constant: 8.14%

Email	Amortization

Loan Amortization: Using the loan term to enhance your financial strategy. Longer terms can spread out the payments, reducing monthly costs but increasing the total interest paid over the life of the loan. Conversely, shorter loan terms increase monthly payments and give you less cash flow. The goal is to gather more cash flow and acquire more properties.

By carefully selecting the loan terms and understanding how interest rates affect your investment, you can optimize your financial commitments and enhance the profitability of your NNN properties.

Maximizing Benefits with 1031 Exchange

Would you rather pay a couple of hundred thousand dollars in taxes or use that tax money to buy more properties?

We use the 1031 exchange strategy for our NNN mentees looking to defer capital gains taxes and move that into a cash-flowing property. By reinvesting the proceeds from a sale into another property, investors can defer taxes and use the full amount of their equity to invest in another property. This process is not for the faint of heart, so we built a team that can do this for you.

If you own other properties, you may be able to sell them and use a 1031 exchange to shift into an NNN investment property, as long as you know what you're doing. Oftentimes, investors sell their single-family or multi-family investments using a 1031 exchange with a third-party accommodator or other options. Our mentees have found it a pain to move millions around to different companies, so we like to do things differently. We keep everything in one place with one company, giving us the advantage of speed and fewer fees and complications!

Finding the Best Financial Strategy for You

We can do this for you, with you, or you can try this on your own. But consider how this strategy fits into your portfolio. Whether you're leveraging traditional loan options, exploring innovative financing structures like sale-leaseback arrangements, or utilizing tax strategies such as 1031 exchanges, the goal is to enhance your investment's profitability, stability, and cash flow.

Financing NNN properties effectively requires a comprehensive understanding of the available options and the ability to strategically implement them to maximize returns. In our mentorship program, we've streamlined these processes to ensure you have the support and expertise needed to succeed. Whether you are just starting or looking to expand your portfolio, having the right financing strategy in place is crucial for building a sustainable and profitable NNN investment portfolio.

Remember, the ultimate goal is to create a portfolio that provides stable, passive income with minimal management responsibilities. By leveraging the right financing options and understanding the intricacies of loan terms, interest rates, and tax strategies, you can achieve financial freedom and build a robust real estate portfolio that stands the test of time

Chapter 4

Understanding The Different Types Of NNN Tenants

Starbucks, Chipotle, and CVS—ever heard of them? These are your new tenants.

As previously mentioned, they are already on NNN leases. Let's delve into how each type can have subtle differences that will impact your portfolio.

Let's make this clear: these tenants are now YOUR tenants. This is not your business; they don't own the property—you do. They just pay monthly rent to you according to the corporate guarantees they have signed. We'll explore the distinct categories of national tenants, from grocery stores and auto parts retailers to pharmacies and fast-food chains, and illustrate why these tenants provide a shield against economic volatility, ensuring steady cash flows even in times of crisis.

The Strategic Importance of National Tenants

NNN investments are distinguished not only by their structure but also by the quality of their tenants. National tenants—large corporations with widespread brand recognition—offer significant advantages over smaller, local operators. The key benefit is the corporate guarantee, which means that the parent company backs the lease, ensuring rent is paid even if an individual location underperforms. This corporate backing lowers the risk typically associated with property leasing and management, as an investor can rely on the financial strength and stability of a large corporation and its multiple locations rather than the uncertainties of a single business entity.

Different Categories of National Tenants

Here are a few prime examples of the different types of national tenants you can have on a Triple Net Lease deal:

Grocery Stores

Grocery stores are considered highly stable tenants due to the simple fact that everyone needs to eat. Chains like Safeway and Publix offer a dependable revenue stream, backed by strong corporate structures. The ongoing need for physical grocery locations, even in an era of increasing online shopping, supports long-term lease commitments.

- **Examples of Grocery Chains**:
    - Safeway
    - Albertsons
    - Publix
    - Kroger
    - Whole Foods
    - Trader Joe's

Grocery stores provide consistent foot traffic and are recession-resistant. They are fundamental to daily life, ensuring a steady flow of customers regardless of economic conditions. This makes them exceptionally reliable tenants that offer long-term lease stability.

Auto Stores

The auto parts sector has shown resilience across economic cycles, with businesses like O'Reilly and Advance Auto Parts expanding their footprint. Their locations are critical to maintaining the supply chain in auto repair and services, providing a stable tenant base for NNN properties.

- **Examples of Auto Stores**:
    - O'Reilly Auto Parts
    - Advance Auto Parts
    - AutoZone
    - NAPA Auto Parts
    - Pep Boys
    - Carquest

Auto parts stores serve the continual demand for vehicle maintenance and repair, a necessity for vehicle owners. These stores benefit from the non-cyclical nature of vehicle repairs, which are required irrespective of economic health. Their presence in both urban and rural areas guarantees a broad customer base, contributing to the robustness of these tenants.

Pharmacies

Pharmacies are essential service providers, often included in the category of recession-proof businesses. Companies like Walgreens and CVS not only offer health-related retail products but also provide critical healthcare services, making them indispensable tenants.

- **Examples of Pharmacies**:
    - Walgreens
    - CVS Pharmacy
    - Rite Aid
    - Express Scripts
    - Safeway Pharmacy

Pharmacies are critical in healthcare infrastructure, providing stability and resilience as they continue to operate even in downturns. They also draw regular customer visits for prescription refills and health consultations.

Quick Service Restaurants (QSRs)

Fast-food chains are popular for their consistent customer traffic and recession-resistant business models. QSRs offer quick and affordable meal options, appealing to a broad demographic. Their business model is designed for high-volume sales, ensuring frequent customer turnover and consistent revenue streams.

- **Examples of QSRs**:
    - McDonald's
    - Burger King
    - Chick-fil-A
    - Taco Bell
    - Wendy's
    - KFC
    - Popeyes
    - Chipotle
    - Subway
    - Domino's Pizza

Day-Care Centers

Day-care centers meet a crucial societal need, providing stability through service-based tenancy. With more families having dual incomes, the demand for childcare services remains high, making these centers a necessity in many communities. They typically have long-term leases to ensure continuity of service.

- **Examples of Day-Care Centers**:
    - Kiddie Academy
    - Learning Care Group
    - The Goddard School
    - Primrose Schools
    - Bright Horizons
    - Tutor Time
    - Childcare Network

- The Learning Experience
- KinderCare

Coffee Shops

Coffee shops serve as modern-day essentials, with locations often featuring long-term leases and high customer loyalty. Their strong brand presence and consistent foot traffic make them excellent tenants for NNN properties.

- **Examples of Coffee Shops**:
    - Starbucks
    - Dunkin'
    - Peet's Coffee
    - Tim Hortons
    - Caribou Coffee
    - Dutch Bros. Coffee

Coffee shops are frequented daily by a loyal customer base and are often considered recession-resistant. Their small-format stores can easily fit into various locations, enhancing their appeal.

Industrial Tenants

Industrial tenants operate on a scale that demands vast, sophisticated spaces such as distribution centers and warehouses. These tenants bring long-term leases and significant investments in the properties they occupy, making them highly desirable for NNN investments.

- **Examples of Industrial Tenants**:
    - Amazon
    - FedEx
    - UPS
    - DHL
    - XPO Logistics

The functionality of these spaces, coupled with the tenants' integral roles in global logistics and e-commerce, ensures a steady demand, providing NNN investors with a buffer against market fluctuations and economic downturns.

Banks and Financial Institutions

Banks typically occupy premium locations that maintain or increase in value, and their leases often include built-in rent escalations, enhancing the investment's profitability over time. Their presence brings a level of prestige and stability, signifying financial strength and long-term tenancy.

- **Examples of Banking Tenants**:
    - Wells Fargo
    - Bank of America
    - Chase
    - Citibank
    - U.S. Bank

The Advantages of National, Corporate-Backed Tenants

The most significant advantage of having national, corporate-backed tenants is the reliability of the cash flow. Unlike smaller, mom-and-pop operations, national tenants offer financial stability thanks to their extensive market presence and corporate support. This means that regardless of the economic conditions, the rent checks keep coming, minimizing the risk typically associated with real estate investments.

The true test of any investment is its performance during times of crisis. NNN properties, with their strong corporate tenants, have proven to be resilient even during global disruptions like the COVID-19 pandemic. While other real estate sectors, such as multifamily and single-family residential, grappled with rent breaks and vacancies, many NNN properties continued to operate and generate income, underscoring their role as the pinnacle of real estate investments.

As we explore the various types of national tenants available for NNN investments, it becomes clear why these investments are considered the holy grail of real estate. The ability to secure properties with corporate-backed leases not only mitigates risk but also ensures a stable, predictable income stream. This chapter has highlighted the critical importance of choosing the right tenants and utilizing professional brokers to secure these optimal investments, setting the stage for financial success and stability in the ever-evolving real estate market.

By prioritizing national tenants with corporate guarantees, investors can transcend the typical challenges of real estate investing, achieving a level of security and profitability that is unmatched by other investment avenues. This strategic approach, coupled with the insights and tactics discussed in this chapter, will empower investors to navigate the NNN investment landscape with confidence and precision.

Chapter 5
Embrace Zero Landlord Responsibilities

What if you could own a property with no landlord responsibilities? Sounds too good to be true, right?

Well, with the right strategies and execution, it could become your reality.

Triple Net Lease (NNN) properties stand out for their unique feature: zero landlord responsibilities. This chapter demystifies what this means in practical terms and explores how it positions NNN investments as some of the most attractive options in the real estate market. With expert guidance and strategic partnerships with experienced brokers or mentors, investors can maximize the benefits of NNN leases, ensuring both stability and profitability, again, with ZERO landlord responsibilities. Think of the net. Whoever is caught by the net is responsible.

The Core Concept of NNN Leases

At the heart of every NNN lease is the concept that the tenant assumes all responsibilities traditionally shouldered by property owners. This includes:

- **Net Operating Income (NOI)**: The rent paid by the tenant translates directly into the landlord's income, free from most usual deductions. This is what the landlord actually earns, making it a pure measure of investment return.
- **Property Taxes**: Typically, a landlord's responsibility, in an NNN lease, tenants manage and pay property taxes directly, ensuring they are never a burden on the investor.

- **Insurance Premiums**: Tenants handle and fund their own insurance coverages, safeguarding the property against potential liabilities and damages.
- **Maintenance and Repairs**: From structural concerns to aesthetic upkeep like landscaping and exterior appearances, tenants maintain the property at their own expense.
- **Operating Expenses**: All costs associated with day-to-day operations, including utilities and any necessary repairs, are managed by the tenant.
- **Compliance**: Tenants ensure that the property meets all zoning regulations and building codes, mitigating legal risks for the landlord.

What Does "Zero Landlord Responsibilities" Really Mean?

If you do not have to take care of anything, what do you call that? We call that freedom at Havrilla Investment Group, allowing investors to enjoy the perks of property ownership without its typical hassles. This arrangement not only simplifies property management but also enhances the predictability of cash flows, as the income received from the property is not diluted by unexpected expenditures or maintenance issues.

Most investors in real estate face unexpected pains like maintenance issues, late rent payments, and property taxes. With an NNN lease property, you will not have to deal with these things. Investors can focus more on strategic growth rather than operational management, making NNN leases particularly appealing to those looking to expand their portfolios without extending their on-ground management commitments.

Working with a Triple Net Mentor can be transformative in navigating the NNN market. We provide invaluable insights into selecting the right properties, negotiating favorable lease terms, and ensuring that tenants are both credible and financially stable. This guidance is crucial in avoiding common pitfalls and securing deals that align with long-term investment goals.

Practical Scenarios of Zero Responsibilities

Consider the scenario where an investor partners with a seasoned NNN broker to acquire a property leased to a national pharmacy chain. With a robust corporate guarantee, the lease ensures a steady Net Operating Income (NOI), immune to common market fluctuations. The pharmacy chain handles all responsibilities, from property tax payments to maintaining the HVAC systems. This means zero unexpected costs for the landlord.

Another example might involve a bank like Chase or Bank of America, where the terms of the lease include the bank's responsibility for all property-related expenses. These tenants not only bring financial robustness but also a high degree of operational discipline, ensuring the property is maintained at a standard that supports their corporate image.

The Bigger Picture

The overarching benefit of NNN investments lies in their stability across economic cycles and the reduced risk because the corporate tenant is covering the cost of the property even if costs fluctuate. By eliminating the unpredictability of property management responsibilities, investors can rest easy knowing that the money is coming in at the end of the day. This, coupled with the right expert guidance, ensures that NNN leases are not just investments in real estate but also investments in financial peace.

In today's world, finding "financial peace"—where you never have to worry about where your money is going—is rare. With NNN leases, you have a clear plan for growth, and you can rely on the corporate guarantee. Zero landlord responsibilities in an NNN lease translate to minimal involvement with maximum returns—an ideal setup for investors seeking to leverage the real estate market without the traditional burdens it carries.

With the strategic use of experienced brokers or mentors, investors can tap into the best of what NNN investments have to offer, making them a cornerstone of a well-diversified investment portfolio. In this era of real estate, where efficiency and effectiveness are prized, NNN investments shine as beacons of opportunity, promising both security and profitability in an unpredictable world.

Embracing the Benefits of NNN Investments

Imagine you own a portfolio of NNN properties leased to high-profile national tenants like Starbucks, CVS, or Chipotle. Each property operates seamlessly, with the tenant handling all operational aspects. As the landlord, your role is largely to collect rent checks and monitor the performance of your investments. This hands-off approach allows you to focus on expanding your portfolio, engaging in new investment opportunities, or simply enjoying the financial freedom that comes with predictable, stable income streams.

The Role of Strategic Partnerships

Partnering with experienced brokers or mentors who specialize in NNN investments can significantly enhance your investment strategy. These professionals bring a wealth of knowledge and industry connections, ensuring you find the best properties with the most reliable tenants. They can guide you through complex negotiations, help structure favorable lease terms, and provide ongoing support to maximize your investment returns.

Case Studies: Successful NNN Investments

Case Study 1: National Retail Chain

An investor acquires a property leased to a national retail chain under a 20-year NNN lease. The tenant is responsible for all property-related expenses, including taxes, insurance, and maintenance. Over the lease term, the investor enjoys steady cash flow and peace of mind, knowing that the corporate-backed lease ensures consistent income. The retail chain's strong brand and financial stability further enhance the investment's security.

Case Study 2: Financial Institution

Another investor secures a property leased to a major financial institution. The lease includes built-in rent escalations, ensuring income growth over time. The tenant maintains the property to high standards, aligning with their corporate image. The investor benefits from the institution's financial strength and long-term commitment, creating a robust, low-risk investment.

Maximizing Returns with NNN Investments

To fully capitalize on the benefits of NNN investments, it's essential to:

- **Select High-Quality Tenants**: Prioritize tenants with strong financial backing and solid business models. Corporate guarantees provide an added layer of security, ensuring rent is paid regardless of individual location performance.
- **Negotiate Favorable Lease Terms**: Work with experienced professionals to secure leases with favorable terms, including rent escalations and long-term commitments.
- **Diversify Your Portfolio**: Spread your investments across various types of NNN properties and tenants to mitigate risk and enhance stability.

NNN investments offer a unique opportunity to achieve financial freedom with minimal management responsibilities. By leveraging the strength of corporate-backed leases and partnering with experienced professionals, investors can build a robust, profitable portfolio. This chapter has highlighted the practical advantages of zero landlord responsibilities, emphasizing how NNN leases can simplify property management while maximizing returns.

In the world of real estate investing, NNN properties stand out as a beacon of stability and profitability. Embrace the benefits of zero landlord responsibilities and unlock the potential of your real estate portfolio. With the right strategy and support, you can achieve financial peace and enjoy the rewards of a well-managed, high-performing investment portfolio.

Chapter 6

Investment Grade Tenants vs. Non-Investment Grade Tenants

Understanding the distinction between investment grade and non-investment grade tenants is one of the most critical aspects of Triple Net Lease (NNN) investments. This knowledge not only impacts the stability and reliability of cash flows but also significantly influences the long-term value of the property. Engaging with a mentor or an expert Triple Net Lease broker is invaluable in navigating these classifications, ensuring you secure deals with the most reliable tenants.

The Importance of Tenant Grades

Having a mentor in this space is essential for a clear understanding of tenant grades. There are certain nuances to navigate, such as ensuring that the national tenant is truly investment-worthy. This might sound surprising, given the emphasis on national tenants up to this point, so let's clarify any potential confusion. Just because there is a national tenant brand name on the lease does not automatically mean they are corporately backed. This distinction is crucial, as it can be a major risk factor if overlooked.

Investment Grade Tenants

Investment grade tenants are those with high credit ratings from reputable credit rating agencies like Moody's, Standard & Poor's (S&P), and Fitch. These ratings reflect the tenant's financial stability and creditworthiness. Properties leased to investment-grade tenants are highly sought after due to their lower risk and reliable income streams.

Characteristics of Investment Grade Tenants:

1. **High Credit Ratings**: Typically rated BBB- or higher by S&P or Baa3 or higher by Moody's.
2. **Financial Stability**: Strong financial statements showing consistent profitability and liquidity.
3. **Corporate Guarantees**: Leases are often backed by the corporation, ensuring rent payments even if a specific location underperforms.
4. **Market Position**: Dominant market presence with a proven business model.

Credit Rating Scales by Agency, Long-Term

Moody's	S&P	Fitch	
Aaa	AAA	AAA	Prime
Aa1	AA+	AA+	High grade
Aa2	AA	AA	
Aa3	AA-	AA-	
A1	A+	A+	Upper medium grade
A2	A	A	
A3	A-	A-	
Baa1	BBB+	BBB+	Lower medium grade
Baa2	BBB	BBB	
Baa3	BBB-	BBB-	
Ba1	BB+	BB+	Non-investment grade speculative
Ba2	BB	BB	
Ba3	BB-	BB-	
B1	B+	B+	Highly speculative
B2	B	B	
B3	B-	B-	
Caa1	CCC+	CCC	Substantial risk
Caa2	CCC		Extremely speculative
Caa3	CCC-		Default imminent with little prospect for recovery
Ca	CC	CC	
	C	C	
C	D	D	In default
/			
/			

WOLFSTREET.com

Non-Investment Grade Tenants

Non-investment grade tenants, on the other hand, have lower credit ratings and are considered higher risk. These tenants may still be national brands but lack the financial robustness and stability of their investment grade counterparts. Properties leased to non-investment grade tenants can offer higher yields but come with increased risk.

Characteristics of Non-Investment Grade Tenants:

1. **Lower Credit Ratings**: Rated below BBB- by S&P or Baa3 by Moody's.
2. **Financial Uncertainty**: Inconsistent profitability and potential liquidity issues.
3. **Lack of Corporate Guarantees**: Leases may not be backed by the corporation, increasing the risk of default.
4. **Market Vulnerability**: Less established market presence and higher susceptibility to economic fluctuations.

The Role of a Mentor

Navigating the complexities of tenant grades is where a mentor becomes invaluable. A mentor can provide insights into:

1. **Due Diligence**: Conducting thorough assessments of potential tenants' financial health and market position.
2. **Lease Negotiations**: Securing favorable terms and ensuring corporate guarantees are in place.
3. **Risk Management**: Identifying and mitigating risks associated with non-investment grade tenants.
4. **Strategic Portfolio Development**: Building a diversified portfolio that balances yield and risk.

Real-World Example

Consider two scenarios:

1. **Investment Grade Tenant**: You acquire a property leased to a high-rated pharmacy chain like CVS. The lease is backed by corporate guarantees, ensuring a stable and predictable income stream. The tenant's strong market position and financial health provide confidence in the long-term viability of the investment.

2. **Non-Investment Grade Tenant**: You purchase a property leased to a lesser-known retail chain with a lower credit rating. While the yield might be higher, the lack of corporate guarantees and financial stability increases the risk of default. This uncertainty can affect the property's value and your overall investment strategy.

Understanding the difference between investment grade and non-investment grade tenants is crucial for successful NNN investing. Investment grade tenants offer reliability and stability, reducing risk and ensuring consistent income. Non-investment grade tenants can provide higher returns but come with greater risk. A mentor or expert broker can guide you through these complexities, helping you make informed decisions that align with your investment goals.

By prioritizing investment grade tenants and leveraging the expertise of seasoned professionals, you can build a robust and resilient NNN portfolio that maximizes returns while minimizing risks.

Chapter 7

Advanced Concepts and Future Steps in NNN Investing

Now that you are familiar with how to buy and hold NNN properties, this chapter explores more sophisticated strategies such as flipping properties and renegotiating leases, which can fetch high five to six figures and sometimes even seven figures. We also delve into the importance of building strong relationships with national tenants and collaborating with a mentor to realize the potential of these advanced investment techniques.

Flipping NNN Properties Using Short-Term Leases

Flipping NNN investments typically involves the strategic acquisition of properties with short-term leases followed by lease renegotiations and a quick resale at a lower cap rate. This approach is distinct from traditional real estate flipping, which often focuses on physical improvements to enhance property value. Instead, NNN flips leverage the financial stability and long-term commitment of quality tenants to increase the property's desirability and market value.

Consider a scenario involving a property leased to a well-known national tenant, such as CVS, with only a few years remaining on the lease. The initial purchase might be negotiated at a better investment opportunity due to the short lease term. An investor with the right expertise and relationships can negotiate an extension of the lease term, transforming the investment's risk profile. Securing a longer commitment from CVS raises the property's value and allows it to be resold at a higher price.

Additionally, you can pull out capital once the new lease has been signed, further enhancing the financial benefits of this strategy.

The Power of Tenant Relationships

The ability to renegotiate leases depends significantly on the relationships owners and investors maintain with their tenants. Previous dealings with tenants like CVS can provide leverage in negotiations, offering more favorable purchase prices and terms. This prior rapport facilitates easier discussions around lease extensions and other beneficial arrangements.

Dark Sites Investment Strategy

Investing in dark sites—properties vacated by previous tenants—presents another opportunity for savvy investors. With a guaranteed corporate lease still in place, investors can negotiate with new tenants to take over the lease under similar or improved terms. This strategy requires a mentor and is an advanced approach that can produce significant capital gains.

Building Relationships and Strategic Partnerships

Strong relationships with tenants and strategic partnerships with mentors and brokers are key to successful NNN investments. These relationships help navigate complex negotiations and secure favorable terms, ensuring the longevity and profitability of your investments.

The Role of Mentorship in Advanced NNN Strategies

Collaborating with a seasoned mentor can be transformative in realizing the potential of advanced NNN investment techniques. A mentor provides invaluable insights, helps avoid common pitfalls, and ensures that each step of the investment process is optimized for maximum returns.

Example Scenarios of Advanced Strategies

Scenario 1: Lease Renegotiation

An investor acquires a property leased to a national retail chain with three years remaining on the lease. By leveraging their relationship with the tenant, the investor negotiates a ten-year extension. This extension reduces the investment's risk and significantly increases the property's market value, allowing the investor to sell at a substantial profit.

Scenario 2: Dark Site Reinvestment

An investor identifies a dark site previously leased to a major retailer. Despite the vacancy, the corporate lease remains active. The investor negotiates a new lease with a different national tenant, securing similar terms. This strategy revitalizes the property, maintains a steady income stream, and enhances the overall portfolio value.

Future Steps in NNN Investing

For those investors keen on taking their real estate ventures to the next level, a consultation with Havrilla Commercial Investment Group is an opportunity not to be missed. Delve into the world of advanced NNN strategies meticulously tailored to your unique needs. This is not just about meeting your investment goals; it's about exceeding them with the finesse of a maestro conducting a symphony.

Imagine the immense potential of your investment portfolio when you join forces with the seasoned experts at Havrilla Commercial

Investment Group. It's about smashing through your investment goals and setting new standards for success.

Conclusion: Transforming Your Portfolio

For investors ready to elevate their real estate ventures, advanced NNN strategies offer a pathway to significant returns and portfolio growth. By building strong tenant relationships, leveraging strategic partnerships, and embracing mentorship, you can transform your investment approach and achieve unparalleled success.

Don't just watch others succeed—be the investor who sets new standards. Schedule your consultation today and transform your portfolio into a powerhouse of performance and profit. Take the step today: Head to triplenetbook.com/book-a-call and schedule your complimentary consultation.

Conclusion
Seizing Control in the World of NNN Investing

As we draw the curtain on our fascinating journey through the world of Triple Net Lease (NNN) investments, it's time to pause and marvel at the unique advantages they offer. NNN investments effortlessly remove many of the headaches traditionally associated with real estate, presenting a smoother, more predictable path to managing your investments and reaping steady returns.

In the realm of NNN investing, you transfer the usual landlord burdens—property taxes, insurance, and maintenance—to your tenants. This isn't merely about lightening your load; it's a transformative shift in your role. You evolve from a day-to-day manager to a strategic investor, focusing on grander opportunities rather than mundane maintenance tasks.

Picture this: investing becomes as straightforward and dependable as collecting dividends from a blue-chip stock. With NNN investments, your tenants—often stable, well-known companies—handle the intricacies of property management. This arrangement ensures your income stream is as consistent and reliable as a Swiss timepiece.

While navigating the NNN investment landscape might seem daunting, you don't have to embark on this journey alone. Partnering with seasoned mentors can be a game-changer. These professionals bring a wealth of market knowledge, strategic insights, and invaluable connections, turning a good investment opportunity into an amazing one.

Imagine the advantage of having a seasoned professional by your side when making investment decisions. They can help you identify the right properties, negotiate favorable lease terms, and manage tenant relationships. It's like having a skilled co-pilot expertly guiding you through the market's twists and turns.

If you're ready to embrace a hands-off approach while still growing your investments, NNN leasing could be your ideal solution. Perfect for those who wish to invest in real estate without the traditional hassles, and with the right support from experienced experts, you can refine your investment strategy and achieve even greater returns.

So, are you ready to elevate your investment game and explore the full potential of NNN investments? Don't let this opportunity pass you by. Schedule a time with my team today for tailored advice and insights aligned with your financial goals.

Take the plunge: Visit `[triplenetbook.com/book-a-call]` (https://triplenetbook.com/book-a-call) and schedule your complimentary consultation. Transform your investment strategy and watch your portfolio flourish.

Printed in the USA
CPSIA information can be obtained
at www.ICGtesting.com
LVHW070858130924
790870LV00001B/12